WITH LOVE...

STEVEN OVERBY

With Love...
Copyright © 2026 by Steven Overby.

MILTON & HUGO L.L.C.
1001 3rd Avenue West, Suite 430
Bradenton, FL 34205, USA

Website: *www. miltonandhugo.com*
Hotline: *1- 888-778-0033*
Email: *info@miltonandhugo.com*

Ordering Information:
Quantity sales. Special discounts are granted to corporations, associations, and other organizations. For more information on these discounts, please reach out to the publisher using the contact information provided above.

Library of Congress Control Number: 2026902148
ISBN-13: 979-8-89285-793-2 [Paperback Edition]
979-8-89285-794-9 [Digital Edition]

Rev. date: 01/12/2026

With love.........

Comes every single emotion imaginable. It is the only thing in this universe that is connected to every emotion. Be it happiness or sadness. It can lift you up or bring your world crashing down around you. It can cause you to hate something but in the very next moment you are showing forgiveness. It can bring countless smiles or tears falling for what seems forever.

It can't be forgotten. It can stand the test of time. It can live on even when time stops. It's the one thing everyone searches for. It is what dreams are made of and what keeps us going when times are tough.

You can't choose who you fall in love with. That's something your heart chooses. It is something that has tried to be explained since the beginning of the first words written. That's what makes it so special because it can't be explain sometimes but once you feel it. You know, god how you know. You can feel it in your heart and people can see it in your eyes.

With love is just the words of how my heart with through so many emotions when it found the one person I could not see myself without.

You didn't know
That it was you
I was holding on to
When you were holding
On to me
Giving me everything
I didn't know I needed
Showing me
What it meant
To hold on to
what I thought
Was just a dream
Holding my hand
Leading me out
The darkness
Showing me the light
To get through
With just the
Look in your eyes
Loving me
When I found
It hard to love myself
Believing in all
That is good

When I didn't think
I could
I will always be grateful
I will always try
With everything in me
To show you
That you are the reason
My heart even beats

I will love you
With the beat
Of 1000 hearts.
Holding you
Every moment
As i watch time stand still
Reaching for only
Your hand
Loving you
With everything I have
Having you believing
Giving everything
That is needed
To show you
To give you
To hold you
With everything in me
To love you
To love only you
From this moment
From this day
Forever
And always

The words of always
Play through my heart
Why does it hurt so much
When we are apart
Your hand in mine
My heart in yours
The moments frozen in time
All play through my head
It's you that need
It's us I want
That's with everything I believe
But tears still fall
Even when you don't see
It's your name I call
To try to get you to me
I stumble, I fall
My head in my hands
But through it all
I can't give up
I can't stop myself
In my arms is where I want you
Fighting with everything in me
I never giving this much
Because I can't see
Me with out you
I feel pieces of me breaking
But each day I put them back together

I find the strength to make it
Just to tomorrow
Just to get to the next day
I knew it from the start
Of what it would take
How it would bring me
To my knees but I can't break
I find a way
I look in my heart
I search every memory
Because that's where you are
I can't walk away
I am giving everything in me
Every single word I say
Every tear that has to fall
Is to fight for love
To give you my all
Put it all out there
To let you know me
To hear
Sally I love you
God how I love you

Some days I believe
With everything in me
Other days our love has
Me on my knees
Begging you not to go
Hoping you will just stay
My hand reaching out
My tears falling down
I can't get you to me
I can't make you see
What our love is doing
To what I once believed
Your promises echo
Through my heart
Each word filling up
Each hole you left
When you walk away
But as you leave
So do the promises
Telling me things
I want to hear
Telling me things
That will happen
But yet you still
Won't tell the truth
You still go home to him
And leave me all alone

Forever is what you say
Always you just can't do
Needing you has left
Me with my heart on the floor
Trying not to break
Trying to hold on
Giving everything I have
In me to you
My words bleed through
The night
My tears burn through
The cold
Wanting just you
Loving you
God with everything in me
I just want you to be mine
But fate hadn't stepped in
Dreams are just memories
That I have created of us
My heart trembles
My hand shakes
Because I know you
Are leaving
And I'll be with out
The one person I will
Ever love

My heart wasn't beating
It was hidden away
Until you found it
Causing it to beat again
My words
Were silenced
Until your kiss
Breathed life back into me
And gave me a reason
My eyes were closed
Lost in the darkness
Until your smile
Opened them and I saw
The light in your eyes
My dreams
Were faded and shattered
Until you held me
And put them back together
My hands
Were weak
Until yours touched them
Giving them strength
To hold on
I stop believing

Many years ago
Until your love
Reminded me
There is a heaven
Because it's
Right here with you

Who knew
One moment
One sentence
One look
Could change my whole world
Who knew
One touch
One kiss
One hug
Would be the only thing I desired
Who knew
One voice
One smile
One laugh
Would become my happiness forever
Who knew
One day
One dream
One girl
Would become everything I loved

I could not write
The words
If it was not for
Your hand
Guiding them
I wouldn't be able
To see
Because it's the
Light in your eyes
That shines through
The darkness
My heart would
Just exist
But it's your love
That breaths
The life into it
I could only
See my dreams
When I closed my eyes
But every time
I look at you
I know they are
Right in front of me
I didn't know
What forever was
Until I held
You in my arms

I couldn't imagine
Loving someone
With everything
In me
Until the day I met you.

Sometimes in life you try to figure out your place in the world. Trying to figure out the person you want to be. But as many find out it is hard. Because most people are always feeling like they are missing something. Like a piece of yourself is lost. That you know you are not whole.

That your heart just doesn't beat the way it should. That the colors of the world are just dim. That the breeze of the wind is just colder than it should be. It's just always something not quite right. But many never figure it out. I didn't know myself.

Until you. Until you walked into my world. I knew then that it was you I was missing. That it was you I needed. I never knew how much was missing until you helped me find every single part of me. That I didn't know I was never truly smiling until you looked at me. I didn't know love until you touched my hand. I didn't know how much I could miss one person so much until you weren't around. I didn't know my heart could dream of so many things until I met you. I didn't know what I would become in this world until you loved me.

For that I will always be thankful. I will always be grateful. And I will always love you.

I was lost in myself
Until you grabbed
My hand
Taking my faded dreams
Bringing them back to the light
Revealing a part of me
I always kept
Hidden in the dark
Giving me everything
I wished for
before I even knew
What I needed
Showing me
My words I wouldn't speak
Just by the
Way you looked at me
The beautiful moments
I once created
In my thoughts
Many years ago
Were brought back
To life
By that one kiss
From that first time
I knew
There was something
About you

But I never imagined
The love
That would flow
Through my veins
How it would
Consume me
To my very soul
How your love
Would breath
The life back into my heart
That had once stopped beating
Filling it with hope
And dreams
And endless possibilities
It's you.
It will always be you
That I will love
In this moment
In this life
Forever and always

Even before your hand
Was in mine
I felt your touch
Running through
All the memories
Yet to be made
Even before I heard
Your voice
I swear I would hear
It echoing through the night
calling out my name
Even before the
First I love you
Left your lips
I knew
With everything in me
You were in every dream
Everything I believed
Everything I needed
You were all I could see
Even before you knew me
I could hear
The words
Beating through my heart
Even before you put
Your hand on my chest
I was holding on

To you
Even before
I fell into your arms
Knowing I would
Never want to let you go
Even before
I looked in to
Those beautiful green eyes
And saw the light in them
That could take away
Everything that was dark
In those world
Even before that first moment
You walked into my life
And changed it for the better
I knew, I knew with everything in me
I would love you, god how I would love you

Wishing you were here
To hold you in my arms
Holding onto you with everything
I have in me
Because I never want
To let you go
Hoping for daylight
Because that's when I'll
See you again
Missing you more
Than I could ever say
Because I just
Can't get the words
To come out just right
Dreaming of you
To keep my close
When you are
So far away
Giving my all
Just to get to us
To get you to me
So our forever can finally start
Loving you with a love
That will burn brightest
Even when all gets dark
Believing in you
Because you are my everything

The reason my heart
Beats each and every day
Needing your touch
Because it is the one
Thing that makes me fell safe
Praying with all that I know
To just make it
These few more months
Because I can
Never see myself
With out you

My heart hesitated
Each time you got close
Until I could feel it beating
Right out my chest
My words stumbled
When I spoke
Because when you looked at me
I found it hard just to breath
When I held your hand
That first time
I wasn't just holding on to you
I was holding on to everything
I would ever need
That first hug
I was shaking
Because I knew
I never wanted to let you go
That first moment
I looked into your eyes
I knew I found
Everything I ever dreamed of
From the first time
I said I love you
I knew way before
That it was you
It was always going to be you
That I could never be with out

As the night falls
Into the cold darkness
And my thoughts get
The best of me
As close my eyes
And I forget
All the times I cried
Because of your love
Surrounding me
With the warmth
Of your arms
Shining through
Like the nights brightest star
Bringing me back
From the loneliness
Giving me
Every single wish
That I could ever
Dream of
Opening up the clouds
So I can see the heavens above
Giving me
The belief
Every single dream
With each moment
You look into my eyes
Your hand

In mine
Not for just today
But for
Every moment after that
Words of your love
Surround my heart
Protecting me
From all that is dark
It's you that makes
Me see
It's you that
Has me believing
It's you that
Has me wanting
The nights
Of you me
Under a trillion stars
As we just
Fall into the love
That will live on no matter
Where we are
That will never fade
Never disappear
That will always
Be true
Far or near
I love you

Some days
My heart is heavier then others
I feel the furthest
Away from you in those moments
That's when I need you the most
But that's the days
I will always say the least
The feelings of loneliness
Feel my soul
The hops of us
No closer than the day before
Trying everything in me
To just get to you
Giving everything
Just to have our love story
I hide the tears
I push them away
Because I can't let you see
How I hate you are not here with me
I hate that you leave me almost
Every night to go there
I feel so helpless
So alone
That's the feeling you don't get
The one you can't understand
The feeling of being lost
When I am around so

Many people
I try to be strong
But it's so hard
Being alone is not what I want
Waking up alone
Each morning
Going to bed alone each night
I don't see the light
I don't see an end
I am trying with everything in me
Not to fall apart
Because I as m the only one
That can fix it
If I want us
I have to be strong
I have to find a way
But it gets so hard
I can't get you to me
I can't get what I want
I can only be alone
I can only hold
My tears in
I can only do so much
Before the weight
Crushes me

I you asked what I want out of life

It would be happiness
It would be unconditional love
It would be laughing for no reason
It would smiling randomly
It would be knowing I can do anything
It would be the memories that last forever
It would the the hearing words that echo through my heart
It would be that one touch that send chills up my spine
It would be a kiss that never ends
It would be knowing everything will be ok
No matter how bad things got
It would be find looking in the future and know without any doubt
that I found everything I could have ever wished for

It's you what I want out of life is you because you make all these
things come true

Yesterday I loved you more
Than all the stars
That shine through the night skies
More than all the grains
Of sand on every beach
Every Desert in this
and every other world
That has have ever existed
More than all the drops
Of water
that has falling
From the heavens
Since the beginning of time
More than all the words
Written in every book
In every song
In every language
That had ever been known
More than you
could ever know
Even if I had forever to show you
Even if I lived a thousand lifetimes
It wouldn't be enough
That was yesterday
But I find myself loving
You even more today

Days come and go
To the point you sometimes forget
Which day it actually is
Sometimes Memories fade away
Because we just don't think about them anymore
Even stars disappear
Into the night to never been seen again
Almost everything in life will
Eventually not exist
Except one thing
My love for you Sally
It can not be measured
It is true and unconditional
It can move mountains if needed
Or pull the stars from the night sky's if you want them
It will shine the brightest
When things seem the darkest
It will hold you close
And keep you safe
It can't be compared to any other love
Because it never existed until you
It is strong enough to stop the world from spinning
It will last beyond forever
It shall never be forgotten
Because it will live on in the heavens above
It will not break or falter no matter what
It is endless and knows no limits

It's a love that will be remembered
Because it's our love story to be written by us

I love you Sally.
I love you with everything in me
Happy birthday
Love Steve

If you looked up at the night sky
You will see it full of stars
Each one different
But yet each one amazingly beautiful
Each night new ones appear
From seemingly nowhere
Many existed long ago
But their light shines on
Because the memory
Of the star is still there
It doesn't fade away
It continues to light the night sky
Each star is a moment
A moment of us
A smile
A laugh
A hug
A kiss
The I love you
The I miss you the most
Each memory we create together
Every moment that we have
Captured in the night sky
As stars that brighten up
Every part of the world

The thoughts of you
Run through my heart
Trying to figure out how
I fell so fast and so hard
And I remember
Each smile you had
As you turned to look me
The way your eyes
Told me everything I needed to see
How my heart was beating
And I couldn't stop
What I was feeling
As your hand brushed
Up against mine
That very
First time
How I knew that moment
I would never be the same
But I didn't know
How much my heart would call your name
I remember the first time
You walked away to leave
And my heart stopped
I knew then
From the tears that were falling
How I needed you
That it stopped me from breathing

The thoughts over taking
Everything in me
The way my heart wanted you
Just to be near
To hold you
In my arms
To calm my fears
I knew at that moment
That I loved you
I knew you could see
How I believed
With everything in me
How I just wanted you
For you to just know
The love I felt
How it was you
That kept
The light in my eyes
From fading away
Into my once lost dreams
My heart is yours
My hope is of us
My belief is of you

If you looked into my eyes
Could you see
All the dreams
I have of you and I

If you held my hand
Would you know
All the words that
I will write
To let you know what you mean to me

If you put your hand
Over my heart
Would you know
That it only exists
Because of you

If you listen closely
Could you hear
All the times
I will tell you
That you are my everything

If you held me close
Would you know
That To me
That I am holding on
To everything I believe in

If I say I love you
Would you know
That I mean
Everyday
Every moment
Every lifetime
Because to me
You are my forever

It was your voice
That whispered in my dreams
Even before that first moment
Before your hand
Even fell into mine
I knew I had felt it before
The words that I have said
Have echoed in my soul
Countless times
Even before you heard them
My heart filled with
A belief of a unmeasurable love
That I knew existed
Because I believed you were always there
The hope of happiness filled my eyes
Even before I saw it in yours
Be it that it was
Always meant to be
Or the love we shared
In our past lives for each other
I knew the moment I held you

That I had held you before
That my heart was yours
Even before I placed it in your hands
Because it was so beautiful and pure
I knew you were the one
Because I fell in love with you
In every moment and every life
That ever existed before

Even if I lived a thousand lifetimes
And traveled to every galaxy
In the known universe
My heart would always
Find a way to yours
No matter the time or distance
Even if I met every person
Who ever lived
I would always choose you
I would choose to be with you
Every single moment
Of every single lifetime
Because I know with everything in me
That it's you that I will always love

Was it when I held you hand
For the first time
And realized yours was the only
One I would ever want in mine

Was it when I looked into your eyes
And could see
The reflection
Of you and me

Was it when the first embrace
Where I was so nervous
And stumbled my words because
You were the only one I saw my life with

Was it the night you left
And I felt like a piece
Of my heart with you too
Because of how I missed you

Was it when the first tear that fell
And I knew
I couldn't ever see
Myself with out you

Was it the first time
I said I love you
Even though I was scared
You wouldn't say it too

Was it the moment
I knew that loosing you
Was the one thing
I couldn't make it through

Even though it was all oh those
I knew it when
The first time you smiled at me
I would never be the same again
Because you had my heart
Right in your hands

As I count the stars above
I think of our love
How it can't be measured
By the number of times
We say I love you
How it can't be one
Single moment that had
Our hearts forever
Linked into each others
It wasn't just that first touch
It wasn't just that first kiss
It wasn't that first tear that fell
When we knew it was the other we missed
It was all those moments
And so many more
It was everything
Every smile
Each time we made each other laugh
The inside jokes
That we only knew
Me stopping in mid sentence
Each time you walked in the room
The way your hand
Would fit perfectly in mine
Each warm embrace
And me not wanting to
Ever let you go

Every time I pulled you close
Every time you told me
I love you the most
The moment you first saw me
With The truest love in my eyes
The times we wondered
Why is it so hard
How we just couldn't walk away
our love wouldn't break
It grew into something
That we both couldn't
Believe was happening
Our love is once
In a lifetime
Once in a thousand years
A love only possible
Because we believed
In everything in our hearts

If I had one wish
I wish you could see
What's in my heart
All the times
That it would skip a beat
As you looked into my eyes
Would you hear
All the words that get lost
When I try to tell
You how much I love you
Would you know
All the times
That I couldn't sleep
Because I missed you
Would you know that
Each day I wake up
I am grateful to have you in my life
Would you know that
It's you a look forward too
Would you understand
That it's your love
That has me wanting
To be better than I was
Would you know
That it's you

That I want until
All the stars have faded away
Would you know that
You are my one
My forever
My always

I thought I knew everything
There was to know
Having all the answers
But I was never asking the right questions
But that all went away
The moment you walked
Into my world
Thinking my eyes were always open
But realized I couldn't see
Until I saw that light
In those beautiful green eyes
My hearting always beating
But it only would stop
When you smiled at me
Causing me to fall to my knees
Because my heart wanted you
The words always there
But never written
Until your hand touched mine
Giving me the courage
To say them out loud
Always the one to fix everything
Always the one people went too when things needed done
The one that never would break
No matter what life threw at me
But I never knew I was broken
Until you showed me the pieces I was missing

Picking up each one and placing them
Back into my heart
Always the one that never had a problem
Sleeping through the night
I could just block out the world and not worry about things.
What ever was going on good or bad
I would just deal with it later
Until you came into my dreams
Filling every single one with your beautiful smile
Keeping me awake each night because you were all I could see
And I knew I couldn't be with out you
Always the one to never ask for anything.
The one to just do it myself
Didn't believe in letting anyone know i needed them
Determined to not to let anyone close
Until you gave me your hand and made me want to say please
don't go.
I need you here with me
Always the loner
Never one to let anyone know me
Keeping everyone away at a distance
Going down every road by myself
But you made it so I couldn't
Breaking through my walls
Having me not wanting to be alone because I just wanted you
near me

I Never knew the meaning of the word I can't
believing I can do anything
Even if no one else thought I could
But for once in my life there is one thing I can't do
I can't see myself with out you
Never one to ever miss anyone
Didn't want to let anyone know I did
So the best way was to just not get close
I never had that feeling where I just needed to see someone so bad
just to get me through the day
But I miss you every single moment even if I just saw you
Not the one to ever wear my emotions on my sleeve
I wasn't going to show my feelings
I didn't want anyone to know what my heart was because that
meant I had to let them in
Until you. Until you. The smiles got bigger, the tears starting falling,
my heart starting believing. I knew then I love you, God how I
love you

The way time
Seems to stop
As you walk into the room
Taking my breath
Away by just looking at me
Leaving me stumbling
Through my words
Trying to find something funny to say
Just to get you to smile
To hear your beautiful laugh
Because when you do
The whole world lights up
Lighting up each moment
With 1000's of colors
That I never knew existed
Filling my heart with
A happiness
That makes it stop beating
Because it's you
It's you, god how it's you
I tried to fight it
But I lost that battle long ago
Because once your hand
Was in mine

I knew I would never let go
I would hold on
With everything I have
Because i knew
Once you walked into
My life
I would never be the same

The words of always
Play through my heart
Why does it hurt so much
When we are apart
Your hand in mine
My heart in yours
The moments frozen in time
All play through my head
It's you that need
It's us I want
That's with everything I believe
But tears still fall
Even when you don't see
It's your name I call
To try to get you to me
I stumble, I fall
My head in my hands
But through it all
I can't give up
I can't stop myself
In my arms is where I want you
Fighting with everything in me
I never giving this much
Because I can't see
Me with out you
I feel pieces of me breaking
But each day I put them back together

I find the strength to make it
Just to tomorrow
Just to get to the next day
I knew it from the start
Of what it would take
How it would bring me
To my knees but I can't break
I find a way
I look in my heart
I search every memory
Because that's where you are
I can't walk away
I am giving everything in me
Every single word I say
Every tear that has to fall
Is to fight for love
To give you my all
Put it all out there
To let you know me
To hear
Sally I love you
God how I love you

Loneliness surrounds me
I try to smile
So no one sees
Each day I fall
Deeper into uncertainty
The light fades
My heart aches
Tears stop
Because my belief
Is failing
I dare not say anything
I can't let you know
That every day my
Heart is breaking
Today I think it's done
But tomorrow it will change
Sadness fills me
From the depths
Of every dream I had
I am trying so hard
I try not to give in
But everything seems so far
I know I am withdrawing
I can't get you to me
And it's killing
Me in every way
I never wanted something

So much
Never needed anyone
With everything in me
But I can't have you
I can't get to you
I just feel so alone

You are my everything
The reason my heart beats
All that I see
Each time I dream
The one who leaves
Me speechless
When you look at me
Taking my breath
Away each time
You kiss me
You are my inspiration
The reason for
the person I become to be
Yours is The
only hand I will hold
Your lips the last
I will ever kiss
The only one I will
Ever love
In the moment
In this life
In everyday
From here until infinity
I spent my nights trying to
To catch the dreams
That danced around in my head
I spent my days

Driving down every road
Trying to find my way
Getting lost
Every time
I was searching
I was wishing
To find everything
I had been missing
But I had stop believing
Giving up
just existing
Until you grab my hand
Spinning my heart
Round and round
Breathing life
Back into me
Picking me up
Off my knees
Showing me
Everything I thought
I would never see
Now I find myself
Loving every moment
Because you
Are right by my side
Giving me
Everything

With just one look
Having my
Heart beating
With the love
That will
Last forever and always

I might be crazy
I might be over dramatic
I might not be your first love
I might not be a lot of things
But I'll be your shoulder
You can cry on
Your hand to hold
When everything seems cold
I'll be here
Giving everything in me
My heart
My love
My strength
I might show my emotions
Just a little too much sometimes
I might withdraw in my thoughts
When I get lost
I might not know everything
But I know it's you
That brings the light into my world
I know Holding on to you
Is the only thing that has me believing
In things that I never thought

Could ever happen
I might be just a guy
In love with a girl
But I know there is a heaven
Because I see it
Every time I look at you

I will love you
Until the last
Star falls
From the heavens above
Holding on
With everything me
Even when all
The water has
Left every ocean
The world could
Stop spinning
And the morning sun
Could Stop rising
I will still be
Loving you
Each day
Every moment
Even when time
Has seem to run out
I'll be here
Still loving you
In this lifetime
And all the ones
That will come

When the days get cold
And the nights get long
I close my eyes
And think of the
First time you walked into my life
That moment forever
Etched in my memories
Because you became
My reason
For everything to believe in
Giving me all I needed
Bringing me to my knees
With your loving
The reason my heart
Started back beating
Breathing life into
My soul
Each time I would hold
You in my arms
Loving me
When I ran out of reasons
To even love myself
Seeing a part of me
That has never be seen
Showing me the meaning
Of what love should be
Having me giving

Everything in me
To always show you
Are my reason for
Believing in
Dreams that I never
Could imagine on my own
Because my reason
To wake up each morning
Is to be loving you
With everything in me
Never giving up
Always trying
Forever showing
Every reason
That has me
Loving everything about you

My heart is
In your hands
Because you
Are all that I am
It's only you
That has ever took
My breath away
Just by looking at me
Showing me things
I thought I would never
Be able to see
Just the moments we share
With each other are forever
Memories that I will
Hold on too
In this life and the next
Your voice
Echos through every
Part of my soul
Giving me hope
Of all that beautiful
In this world
Your hand is all I want
To always be in mine
Because I will hold on
With everything I have
Giving everything in me

To show you
What I believe
Each and everyday
To never stop showing you
That you are the reason
For the things I do
Letting you know
How amazing you are
How I can't ever
See myself loving
Anyone but you

How do you know you are love

Is it the holding hands?

Is it the long embrace that lasts for what seems forever?

Is it the laughing uncontrollably?

Is it the late night talks?

Is it when you look in her eyes?

All of those make you realize you are in love

But it's only one true thing that will make you realize how much

It's when you are in a crowded restaurant

She reaches over and grabs your hand

She proceeds to take your wallet oh so gently.

Opens up said wallet pulls out 20 dollars

Looks you deep into your eyes softly saying

What! Say something!

Then gives you back your wallet with such loving care.

That's the sign that it's the truest love because we have reached
the final stage of a loving relationship. Which is what's mine is hers
♥♥♥♥♥♥

That lets me know this will always be forever

As you look into
The night sky
Into the light of
A billion stars
Each one
Uniquely different
Some shining
Brighter than others
But each night
They are always there
Even if one fades away
Another will takes its place
Time will pass
Memories will be forgotten
But each night
The stars in that
Same night sky
Will always be there
It would take a lifetime
To count each one
It might even take forever
Those stars represent
Each moment with you
Each time I see you
Everything I love about you
And how long I will love you
Forever and always

When my words fade
From the notes
That they were once
Were written
When my last
Thoughts can
No longer be spoken
When my hand
Can no longer
Grab on to yours
When I don't
Have the strength
To pull myself back
Up anymore
When the breath
Leaves my lips
For the last time
When my heart
Can no longer beat
I want you to
Look into
The night sky
And remember
That for every
Star that shines
Is a reason
I fell in love with you

Things I will always give you

My time
My words
My understanding
My laughs
My hand
My strength
My forgiveness
My trust
My dreams
My beliefs
My hope
My heart
My soul
My effort
My praise
My support
My love
My forever
My always
My everything.
Just always know I will give everything in me.
To always show you are my reason for waking up each day and
knowing that today will always be better than yesterday because I
get one more day with you.

In life you make thousands of choices. Some good and some well not so good. But each choice is a path you take. You never know where that path is leading but along the way more choices appear. Which leads you down countless paths. The places you go and the people you meet. You find friends, you find happiness and you sometimes you find heartache.

As you get older you experience so many things down the paths that you assume are just random. But are they really random. Is there some other force that drives us to choose certain things at what you think are random times.

Think about it this way. Look at the one you love. What if one thing changed. What if they never said hello. What if they never moved here. What if they kept their feelings inside and never said anything. Think of so many right and wrong choices that were made to get me to you. Every choice, every path taken, every decision made lead me here with you. Some might say it is luck and that could be true but what if. What if it was already written in my heart and I had to go through everything good and bad. What if my whole life was preparing me to love you. Every decision I made had me finding my way to you. If one thing changed. I wouldn't be here in front of you telling you that you are my one.

As I look at you
I wonder if you know
What I see
It's not just your
Beautiful smile
It's just your
Breath taking green eyes
Its more so much more
I see the reflection
Of every moment
Every time
Your hand touched mine
Every time I held
You in my arms
Knowing it was you
That would become
My whole heart
To see a dream
Come to life
With each time
You look at me
To feel the love

Inside of me
That I never knew
Could be this strong
To know that it's you
It will always be you
That I will reach for
Every day
Every moment
Forever and always

How do you truly know you love someone ?

Is it the happiness they bring in your life? Yes only she can make you smile by just walking in the room. Her voice is something you always want to hear. Her laugh can just make you laugh just by hearing it.

Is it the words that are said? Yes. When she speaks her words hold the most weight. They mean more because you believe in her with everything you have. You trust her with everything because she is your hope.

Is it the way you look at her? Yes. When you look at her you look at her like she is the only one in the world for you because you believe it with everything in you. That In a way you are looking up at her because you know there is no one else that you will ever see with pure love like you do her.

For me though it was all of those but one always hit harder.

Is it when you miss her? Yes. God yes. It's when you feel a piece of you leave every time she walks away. That you get sad because you know she is your best friend, your happiness, and your everything. That you know you are better with her around than when she is not. That the nights get longer because your mind races because you just want her near you. That she is the one you can't see yourself without. Her presence is etched into your heart until it no longer beats. It's doing everything you can to get her to you because you need her. You need her just to breathe some days. To me it's when you miss someone that tells you how much you love them. Because the more you miss her the more you will always appreciate the time you have together. Because that's the one thing that you can never get back is time. When you truly miss someone it is because you are missing the moments with the one you truly love. It's the moments that keep your heart and memories alive. So you miss making memories with her that's why missing her is so hard.

That's how I knew. I knew it the first time I missed you that I didn't ever want to be with out you ever in my life. I knew how I felt. How sad I got and how much I just wanted you here with me.

That's how I know how much I love you because I miss you with everything single thing in me.

If you asked me where my heart is
I would say it was with you
If you asked me what I dream about
I would say it was of you
If you asked where I want to be
I would say right beside you
If you asked why do I believe
It would be each time you look at me
If you asked what's the one thing I can't live with out
The answer would always be you
If you asked what I need
It would be you forever
If you asked me give you a reason of why I love you
The reason is you
You opened up a part of me I never knew.
You give me strength to hold on
You give me hope when it gets dark
You are what I miss because I feel incomplete without your love
I love you I love you with all my heart
That's with everything I believe in
But I also know you love me. I know you do.
I just miss you I miss your smile. I miss your hugs. I miss the smell
of your hair. I miss your hand in mine. I miss your laugh. I miss your
touch. I miss everything about you.

Some people think it's one moment that changes your whole life

but for me

It was one person that changed every moment because I am lucky enough to share them with her

If I could write what's in my heart
I would be writing the rest of my life
If could speak the words
That run through my head
My voice would fade away
All I know is that I could
Tell you I love you
Over and over but
That would not tell you
How I feel
What I feel can not
Ever be explained fully
All I can do is show you
Show you that you are my world
That it's you that gives me
A reason to believe
In my whole life I searched for happiness
I never knew what it could even be
Until I met you.
When I tell you I love you to me it means that
You are my one. My other half because without you I am only half of
who I need to be. I'll never want anyone but you. My heart is forever
in your hands. The belief I have in you is stronger than anything I
could have ever imagined. You are the one i will always look forward
to seeing. The one I will always want by my side. The one I'll give my
all too. The one hand I will ever want in mine. The one I will hold
until my arms give out. It's you Sally. It's you that I love. A love that

burns a hole right through me. I am so grateful for you. So thankful for you. I love you. I love you because you are everything to me. I love you for who you are. I love you and you are the only person I will ever love. I know this because I have never felt or believed in someone like I do you. I know in life they are challenges and I know things will get hard. But I also know I can get through anything but there is only one thing I could never get through that is if I didn't have you. That's the only thing in life that I can't see. I can't see me with out you. You are forever etched in my heart. From the first kiss until my last breath. I will love you with everything in me

Who knew one day
That one person
Would take
My hand
Into theirs
Holding it gently
But with the strength
Of a love
That would
Change my world
Into something
That I once thought
Was just a dream
Giving me everything
By just being
Right here beside me
Showing me the
Greatest thing
Ever imagined
Making my heart
Start beating
With the belief
Of something
That only comes
Around once
In a lifetime
That true love

Does exist
Because of each moment
That you are with me
I know, I know with
Everything in me
That I love you

In my life I believed
Of a love
That would inspire me
To be better
Than I ever thought I could be
A love that isn't
Just about the words
Because they
Just can be something that is heard
It's not just things
That we do to show we care
It's not just the
Holding hands
Or laughing together
It's when I look into
Your eyes
And it reminds
Me of every dream
Every wish
That I ever made
To know it's you
Without any doubt
With out any hesitation
That there is no one else
I could ever see
The way I see you
You are my reason

The one I miss every
Single moment
Because I am
So much better with you
Than I was ever with out you

I feel like I can't take it
My heart is breaking
Inside my chest
To my knees I am falling
The tears burning
A hole through your memories
My words fail
My hand reaches for you
As you turn to walk out that door
Your love is slowly killing me
I don't know what do
I don't know what to say
Knowing your not mine
I know that you have to leave
My heart stops beating
The tears start falling
Your name is all I am calling
But no one hears
Because I just keep it all inside
No one knows
No one sees
The pain of you leaving
Stops me from breathing
It's only you that that needing
But it's the one thing I can't have
So close but yet so fucking far
I try to hold on

I try to not break but only bend
But it's so hard
To see your dreams smiling back at you
To see ever wish in your eyes
To know that you are all I will ever love
Your hand in mine
Your kiss still on my lips
The touch of your skin
Still burned into my finger tips
The want the need
The everything I believe
Is all in you
The love the passion the desire
Burns through my soul
I stumble I fall
Over and over again
I don't know how I got
This far
I don't know how to
Keep from falling apart
My fears my own downfall
Scared of losing you
Afraid you waking up
One day and realize
That you had enough
That it's too much
That it's not worth fighting for

That I was nothing more
Than just someone to broken
Fears consume me
Making me feel so weak
I can't help it
My love is so strong
Just the thought of losing you
Tears my heart out my chest

The reflection of the lights in the dark
Fade as each mile goes by
As I reach for you
All I find is your memory
My heart is in my throat
My tears fall as I close my eyes
All I want is you
But you are so far away
I try to be strong
I try so fucking hard
But I get shaken to my core
Your words echo through the darkness
Your kiss I still taste on my lips
But I am still alone
Waiting hoping for it to be over
Holding on with both hands
But each day I slip and fall
Into the sadness of you not being here
All I dream is us
All I need is your love
But it's so far away
My tears stain your picture
As look through my phone
My words is all have to tell you
How much you I love you
My heart is yours
But i can't have you

Why does this have to be so hard
Why does it hurt so much
Missing you is consuming
My very soul
With out you I can't
Feel whole
I try to pick myself
I try to get the next day
But I stumble and I fall
Into the dreams of you
My heart is yours
Is has been for a long time
All I want is to
Feel your hand in mine
All I want is you
I know I am broken
I know I am not as strong
As I seem
I cant help it my heart is In your hands
And it bring me to my knees somedays
All I dream is the days I can call you mine
All I think of is the memories of each time
I was able to hold you in my arms
Each time I looked in your eyes

And told you what's in my heart
The times I could speak
As I tried to find my words
To tell you how much I love you
To tell you it's nothing
I wouldn't do
To bring you to me

From the first time our eyes met
To our first kiss
On that warm Sunday afternoon
From the first time you smiled at me
To the moment you made me first believe
From all the times we passed each other
To the times we were tangled up in one another
From the first time I made you laugh
To the times I held you in my arms
From the first time I saw love in your eyes
To the first I missed you when we said goodbye
From the moment my hands touched yours
I knew there was nothing I wanted more
From the moment i opened my heart
For you to always be apart
From the moment I told you I loved you
I knew Sally I knew that there was nothing I would do
Just to make more moments with you

My tears burning
My heart trembling
The thoughts of you
Breaking me into
Something so strong
Something that came from a wrong
Turned into in this that is good
But also so much pain
I call out your name
I reach for out for our love
But I feel it all slipping away
All I want is us
With everything I believe
But I can't get you to me
Thousands of words
Flood my heart
But I fill like
My whole world is falling part
I believe in you
I believe in us
But it's getting harder
To make it to the next day
I see the pain in your eyes
As I sit here with tears in mine
Can I walk away
Can I just let it be
God tell me what to do

Help me see
The things I am not able
Give me the strength
To give her what she needs
Give me the courage
To just let her be
I can't have what I want
She is everything I'll ever need
But I just make things worse

What if I never turned around
That day you said those words
What if I never told you
What was in my heart
What if I just let things be
What if is something I couldn't do because
Then I wouldn't be able to see
The love in your eyes
My heart wouldn't be beating
My words was just have drifted away
I would never have known
This love you have given me
I would never have known
What it was like to hold my whole world
In my arms
To believe in someone
That I wished for so long
To have a feeling of love
That will never fade
Even if all the stars fell from above
To feel your hand
Touch the very depths of my soul
Pulling me into your heart

And finding the greatest love ever known
What if is something that
I think about
Because I am so lucky
We found a love we could
Never live without

Some days I believe
With everything in me
Other days our love has
Me on my knees
Begging you not to go
Hoping you will just stay
My hand reaching out
My tears falling down
I can't get you to me
I can't make you see
What our love is doing
To what I once believed
Your promises echo
Through my heart
Each word filling up
Each hole you left
When you walk away
But as you leave
So do the promises
Telling me things
I want to hear
Telling me things
That will happen
But yet you still
Won't tell the truth
You still go home to him
And leave me all alone

Forever is what you say
Always you just can't do
Needing you has left
Me with my heart on the floor
Trying not to break
Trying to hold on
Giving everything I have
In me to you
My words bleed through
The night
My tears burn through
The cold
Wanting just you
Loving you
God with everything in me
I just want you to be mine
But fate hadn't stepped in
Dreams are just memories
That I have created of us
My heart trembles
My hand shakes
Because I know you
Are leaving
And I'll be with out
The one person I will
Ever love

My heart is breaking
My dreams are fading
Wondering how I get you to me
Hoping it's not too late
I feel like giving up
I feel like I am no closer
To what is the dreams of us
The more you tell him
The more I feel you pulling away
His words echo through your mind
Mine silent in your heart
I am left alone
I am left to my fears
When will be over
Why can't the truth be told
Lies just make things worse
Pushing me to the edge
I feel like I am not good enough
I feel like I am not worth that fight
You tell me it will be over soon
But once you get around him
You won't tell the whole truth
I feel like nothing I do gets you
Each night you go home
I pray for the light
I hope tomorrow it will be over
But yet when the phone rings

Nothing has changed
Nothing happened
Just another night
Of my heart breaking
I hit my knees
My head in my hands
Tears fall
I pray for strength
I need you
But I know you will not come
I want to tell you
Please come to me
But I know you want
Even if you say it
I know it's just my wish
I know each night I will
Sleep with just your memories
In my heart

Would you know
Each time the tears fell
The ones you didn't see
When I was all alone
No one to call
No one to tell
Would you know
The nights that
My heart broke
Right into
Would you
Know the nights
I fell into
The thoughts
Of loosing you
The times I wanted
You here with me
The times I picked
Up my phone
But put it back down
Because I know
I have to
Fight these
Tears Alone
How many times I needed you
But you didn't come
Knowing I was breaking
Knowing I was hurting

Lost in my thoughts
Shaken to my soul
Fears of loosing
You take hold
My knees ache
From falling
My heart breaks
It's your name i am calling
Tears stream
Down my face
Burning through
The memories
Of you in my arms
Of your kiss on my lips
Trying to hold on
Trying not to break
As each time my heart
Beats I feel a part of it
Shatter as you walk away
I try to speak I want to just yell
Please stay
Please don't go
But I say nothing
I just smile
Hoping you don't notice
Me breaking right in front of you
Pulling my hat down

So you don't see me cry
Wishing you would turn
Your car around
Wishing you would
Come back to me
Hoping it will be over soon
Praying for tomorrow
To get here
So I can just see you
One more time
Just hold you
To tell you
Don't go

Moments of us
Fading away
My hearts hurts
More than I say
Each night I feel
More alone
Tears fall
Sadness calls
From my lonely heart
I need you but
You are not here
I call for you
But I get no answer
Do you know
My hearts breaking
Do you know
It's now I need you the most
But I left to myself
Wondering if I will break
Hoping I just make it one more day
You say when you get back
That things will be in open
But that's not the truth
It's just what you tell me
Just words to keep me
From falling
Into the darkness

I just wish you
Would just be honest
Just tell the truth
I feel like you
Are more worried
Of him
Then you are of breaking me

My dreams are of us
Holding each other
As our lips touch
Remembering
Like it was the first time
They way our eyes met
So many thoughts in my mind
Who knew that one moment
Would lead to thousands more
That it was meant
To be
Written in the stars
Way before we
Even knew our hearts
Would fall into
This love we have
As I looked at you
On that day
I knew it was
No way
I would ever not give my all
To give you my heart
But I didn't know I would fall
So hard and so fast
I knew you
would be the last
I knew it would be

No one else
That I would ever see
Myself holding onto
Each night
Because it's you
On that day
My heart was yours
Even though I didn't have to say
I knew I would love you
With everything in me
And there was nothing I could do
To stop my feelings
And not did I want to
That's the day I knew
That I would always
Be in love with you

Loneliness surrounds me
I try to smile
So no one sees
Each day I fall
Deeper into uncertainty
The light fades
My heart aches
Tears stop
Because my belief
Is failing
I dare not say anything
I can't let you know
That every day my
Heart is breaking
Today I think it's done
But tomorrow it will change
Sadness fills me
From the depths
Of every dream I had
I am trying so hard
I try not to give in
But everything seems so far
I know I am withdrawing
I can't get you to me
And it's killing
Me in every way
I never wanted something

So much
Never needed anyone
With everything in me
But I can't have you
I can't get to you
I just feel so alone

www.ingramcontent.com/pod-product-compliance
Lightning Source LLC
Chambersburg PA
CBHW051841040426
42447CB00006B/635